21st Century
Basic Skills
Library

KIDS CAN
RECYCLE

by Cecilia Minden, PhD

Cherry Lake Publishing • Ann Arbor, Michigan

3

Published in the United States of America
by Cherry Lake Publishing
Ann Arbor, Michigan
www.cherrylakepublishing.com

Photo Credits: Cover and pages 1 and 14, ©Morgan Lane Photography/
Shutterstock, Inc.; page 4, ©iStockphoto.com/Juanmonino; page 6,
©Diego Cervo/Shutterstock, Inc.; page 8, ©iStockphoto.com/robcruse;
page 10, ©Aaron Amat/Shutterstock, Inc.; page 12, ©Norman Chan/
Shutterstock, Inc., page 16, ©Cary Kalscheuer/Shutterstock, Inc.; page 18,
©iStockphoto.com/Photoservice; page 20, ©iStockphoto.com/Jbryson.

Library of Congress Cataloging-in-Publication Data
Minden, Cecilia.
  Kids can recycle/by Cecilia Minden.
     p. cm.—(Kids can go green!)
  Includes bibliographical references and index.
  ISBN-13: 978-1-60279-867-0 (lib. bdg.)
  ISBN-10: 1-60279-867-2 (lib. bdg.)
  1. Recycling (Waste, etc.)—Juvenile literature. I. Title. II. Series.
  TD794.5.M555 2011
  363.72'82—dc22   2010015732

Cherry Lake Publishing would like to acknowledge
the work of The Partnership for 21st Century Skills.
Please visit www.21stcenturyskills.org for more information.

Printed in the United States of America
Corporate Graphics Inc.
July 2010
CLFA07

TABLE OF CONTENTS

What Can Kids Recycle?

Time to take out the trash!

Wait! Let's see what we can **recycle**.

Recycle means to use something in another way.

5

Glass and paper can be recycled.

Clean all glass **bottles** and jars.

Paper should be dry. **Package** it in clean paper bags.

Plastic can also be recycled. Make sure it is clean.

Be careful of **metal** cans. The lids are very sharp!

How Can Kids Recycle?

Does your family have a place to sort trash?

Help them set up recycling bins.

Use pictures to help you **label** the bins.

Now everyone will know how to sort the trash.

Remind others to recycle.

Check the bins.

Help keep things in the right bins.

Where Can Kids Recycle?

Some towns pick up recycling when they pick up trash.

Put your recycling **containers** by the curb.

17

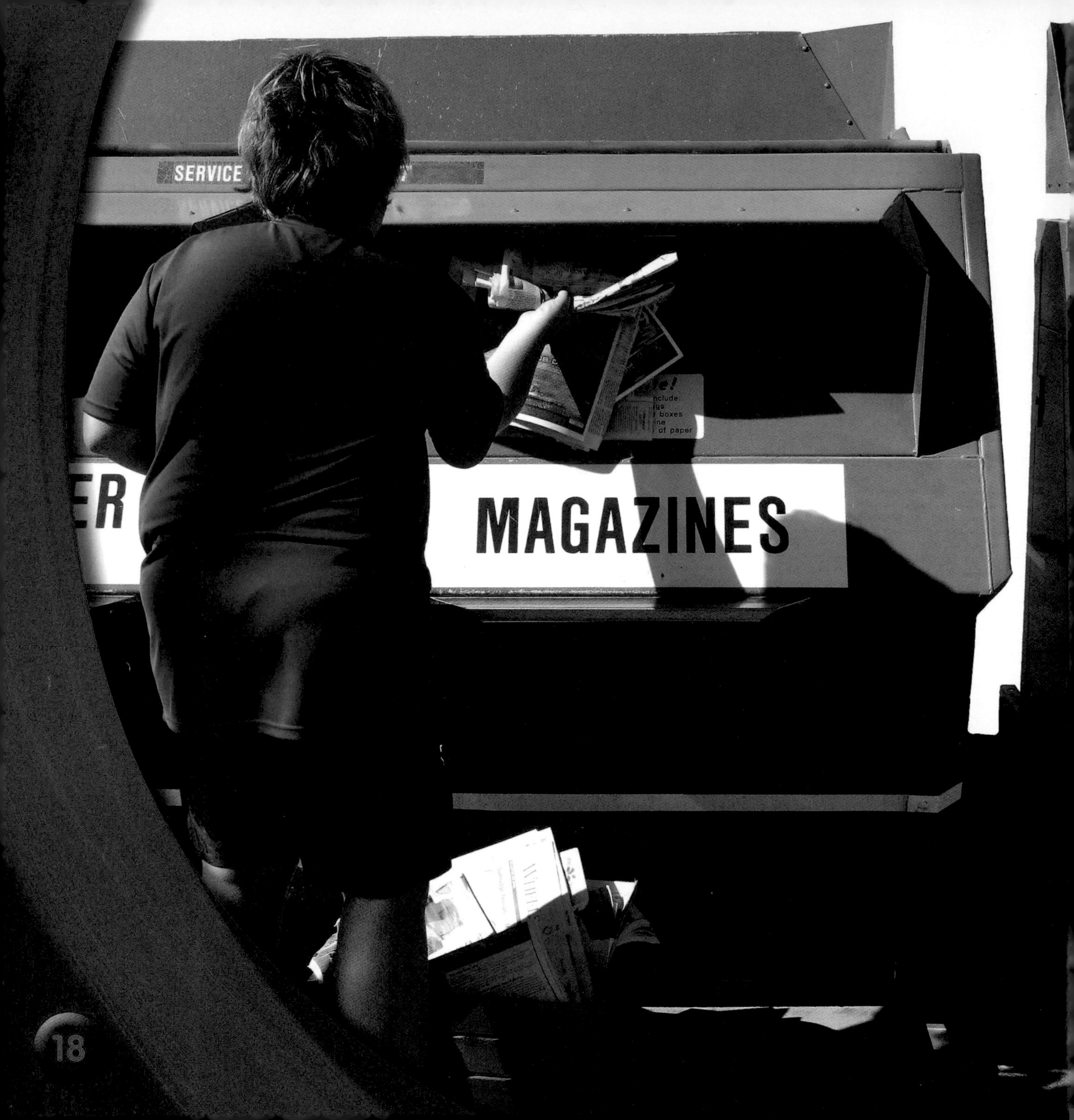
SERVICE
ER
MAGAZINES

Other towns have recycling centers.

People bring their trash to the centers. Everyone sorts their trash and puts it in the big bins.

Recycling helps reduce trash.

It helps save our **natural resources**. It also saves energy and keeps Earth clean.

What will you recycle today?

Find Out More

BOOK
Goldsmith, Mike. *Recycling*. New York: Crabtree Publishing
Company, 2010.

WEB SITE
NIEHS Kids Page—Recycling!
kids.niehs.nih.gov/recycle.htm
Learn more about how you can help protect the environment.

Glossary

bottles (BOT-uhlz) containers that have narrow necks and
mouths; most bottles do not have handles

containers (kuhn-TAYN-erz) boxes, jars, or bottles used to hold things

label (LAY-buhl) to put a word or sign on something

metal (MET-uhl) a material that is usually hard and shiny

natural resources (NACH-ur-uhl REE-sorss-sez) materials found
in nature that are useful to people

package (PAK-ij) to put something into a container

plastic (PLASS-tik) a light, strong material made by humans

recycle (ree-SYE-kuhl) to turn old things into new things

Home and School Connection

Use this list of words from the book to help your child become a better reader. Word games and writing activities can help beginning readers reinforce literacy skills.

a	does	lids	recycled	they
all	dry	make	recycling	things
also	Earth	means	reduce	time
and	energy	metal	remind	to
another	everyone	natural	resources	today
are	family	now	right	towns
bags	glass	of	save	trash
be	have	other	saves	up
big	help	others	see	use
bins	helps	our	set	very
bottles	how	out	sharp	wait
bring	in	package	should	way
by	is	paper	some	we
can	it	people	something	what
cans	jars	pick	sort	when
careful	keep	pictures	sorts	where
centers	keeps	place	sure	will
check	kids	plastic	take	you
clean	know	put	the	your
containers	label	puts	their	
curb	let's	recycle	them	

Index

About the Author

Cecilia Minden is the former Director of the Language and Literacy Program at the Harvard Graduate School of Education. She currently works as a literacy consultant for school and library publishers and is the author of more than 100 books for children.